Oregon's Coas

Canoe & Kayak Guide

By Ron Wardman

Westways Press
Coos Bay, Oregon

Oregon's Coos Region: Canoe and Kayak Guide
By Ron Wardman   Photos by Tom Baake
Copyright © 2001
by Ron Wardman and Westways Press.

Westways Press
440 Third Ct.
Coos Bay, OR 97420

When you travel any of the roads, trails and waterways discussed in this book, you assume responsibility for your safety. Author and publisher assume no liability for accidents and incidents. Author and publisher cannot guarantee accuracy of information and cannot guarantee that tours are suitable for every paddler. Please read important information in the Introduction.

Design consultation, production and printing by Wegferd Printing and Publications, North Bend, Oregon. Printed on recycled paper.

Library of Congress Cataloging-in-Publication Data:

Wardman, Ronald J.
  Oregon's Coos Region: Canoe and Kayak Guide
by Ron Wardman

ISBN: 0-9658012-1-7

1. Outdoor Recreation -- Canoe/Kayak
2. Travel -- Oregon
3. Oregon Coast

CONTENTS

COOS REGION MAP..5

INTRODUCTION..6-9

NORTHERN COOS REGION................................10-25
    Lake Marie..10-11
    Eel Lake..12-13
    Ten Mile Lakes..14-17
    Ten Mile Creek..18-19
    Saunders Lake..20-22
    Beale Lake..23-25

COOS BAY AREA..26-60
    Charleston to Empire..27-28
    Empire to North Spit..29
    North Spit..30-31
    North Spit to North Bend..32
    Pony Slough..33
    North Bend Boat Ramp to Coos Bay..34-36
    Coos Bay to Eastside Boat Ramp..37
    Coos and Millicoma Rivers..38-41
    North (Hauser) Slough..42
    Haynes Inlet..43-45
    Larson Slough..46

SOUTH SLOUGH AREA..47-52
    South Slough..47-51
    Joe Ney Slough..52

OTHER COOS BAY AREA SLOUGHS..53-64
    Coalbank Slough..53-54
    Catching Slough..55-57
    Isthmus Slough..58-62
    Davis Slough..63-64

Contents

COQUILLE RIVER 65-73

    Old Town Bandon to Bullards Beach Park 65-66
    Bullards State Park to Rocky Point Boat Ramp 67
    Rocky Point around Randolph Island 68
    Rocky Point to Riverton Boat Ramp 69
    Riverton to Sturdivant Park 70
    Sturdivant Park to Arago Boat Ramp 71
    Arago Boat Ramp to Myrtle Point 71
    Beaver Slough 72-73

NEW RIVER 74-78

FLORAS LAKE 79-81

OTHER LAKES IN THE REGION 82-92

    Empire Lakes/John Topits Park (Coos Bay Area) 82-83
    Johnson Pond (Coquille Area) 84-85
    Bradley Lake (Bandon) 86
    Garrison Lake (Port Orford) 87-88
    Powers Pond 89
    Ben Irving Reservoir (Winston area) 91-92

GLOBAL POSITIONING SYSTEM (GPS) COORDINATES 93

HELPFUL PHONE NUMBERS 93

AUTHOR'S NOTES 94

PUBLISHER'S NOTES AND PHOTO NOTES 95

READER'S NOTES 96

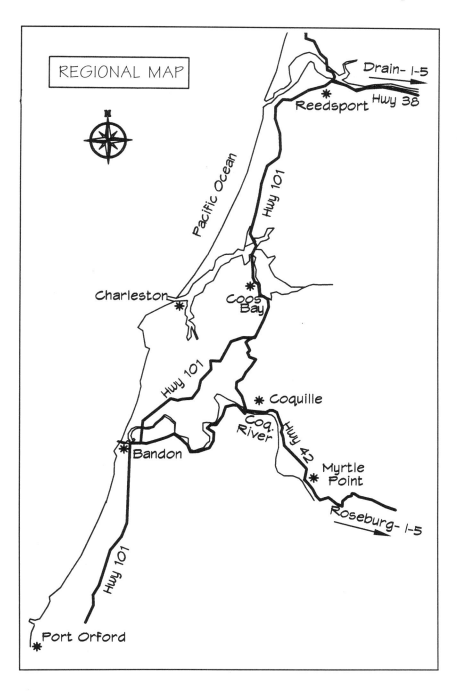

INTRODUCTION

I've been having a lot of fun over the past few years exploring places to paddle the inland waters along Oregon's South Coast. There are literally dozens of paddling opportunities — from lakes and streams in the Oregon Dunes, to the estuaries of Coos Bay and the Coquille River, to the lakes and rivers south of Bandon.

In my travels I've seen many people carrying canoes and kayaks on their vehicles' roof racks, but they seldom seem to stop. Figuring that perhaps people weren't aware of the many places to paddle in this region, I decided to gather the basic information about various paddling spots and make some photocopies to pass around. A few enthusiastic friends later convinced me that the subject deserved a "real" guidebook, complete with maps and photos.

This book offers both saltwater and freshwater tours that were selected for their relatively easy paddling. You won't find information about whitewater paddling or open-ocean kayaking. Nor is this a comprehensive nature and historical guide of the area. Most paddlers are observant and appreciate their surroundings without a great deal of outside help.

I need to make the usual disclaimers associated with paddling:

WARNING!

Paddling is potentially a dangerous sport. Lives can be lost when paddlers don't follow safe paddling guidelines. You must know and respect your skill level.

Paddlers should always be aware of weather, tides, and currents. All of the waters of this region can be **cold**, with temperatures ranging between 45 and 60 degrees. **If you are immersed, hypothermia and death can quickly follow**.

While these trips are relatively easy, you must be realistic regarding your skill level. Try to paddle with a partner. Consider carrying a two-way VHF radio or cell phone.

Always carry proper emergency equipment and wear approved flotation devices. Flotation devices are mandatory in Oregon for children 12 years old and younger at all times in watercraft.

Always use caution when entering any water in an open boat or canoe. Do not enter surf, bays or other bodies of water during storms or heavy chop.

Some of these trips are in working waterways, so watch out for ships, tugboats, barges and log rafts. They all create a significant water disturbance that can easily swamp such open watercraft as canoes.

Because water levels vary greatly, always be on the lookout for hazards just below the surface. Partially-submerged floating logs — called "deadheads" — are common in local waters.

During winter and early spring, heavy amounts of rainfall can add a great deal of water to the area, influencing currents and water levels. Winter storms bring strong south winds, which are usually short-lived. That said, keep in mind some of the best paddling is actually in winter and spring; between storms, calm and warm days can occur.

Summer, on the other hand, sees strong north winds arriving nearly every afternoon. Try to plan exposed trips for the mornings.

A WORD ABOUT THE TIDES

Many of the areas discussed are tide-dependant. You should obtain a tidebook (available at many local stores) and use the corrections, if any, for the places where you're paddling. Local newspapers also daily print tide charts.

When the term "high tide" is used in this book, it refers to the time of high tide at the Coos or Coquille river channel entrances at the Pacific Ocean. As you go "upriver" in the Coos and Coquille estuaries, the time of high tide time is later in respect to how far upriver you travel. The farthest reach of tidewater — called the "head" of tidewater — is roughly 30 miles on each river system, and is two to four hours later than high tide time at the mouths of each river.

If you're paddling on an outgoing tide, be sure you know where the channel is, since you could get caught on mudflats as the tide falls. The mudflats consist of sticky ooze that's not much fun to wade through! This is particularly true in the South Slough, in the Coos Bay channel between North Bend and Coos Bay, and up Catching Slough.

Most tidal inlets and sloughs have steep embankments that become exposed as the tide goes out. This makes it difficult to get in and out of small craft.

I've tried to note the approximate calculations for determining high tide or low tide, but land observations should always be made prior to paddling. Each trip as described takes advantage of tides and currents. In determining tides and currents, I used the software program ChartView with its companion Tides and Currents.

Put-in/take-out sites and information

Each tour notes the best place to launch, general information about the direction of the tour, unusual hazards, the length of the trip and approximate time for the trip.

I used a global positioning system (GPS) device to determine the distance of each tour, which is less than the actual shoreline mileage or, in the case of lake paddles, the shoreline perimeter. Actual perimeter mileage of lakes is shown in parenthesis when known.

A note about the maps: Because of their small size, the maps include only the most obvious details. They are correct to scale and reasonably accurate. I have widened waterways and rivers in some instances for clarity.

Paddling times are approximate times based on fairly easy paddling, with time for observing points of interest. Each trip is based on starting from and returning to the same place unless noted otherwise. However, many of the trips in the sloughs and bays could be one-way if you have a second vehicle to work out a shuttle.

I hope you have a safe and enjoyable time exploring the many watery delights of the Coos Region!

Local paddler Frank Babcock guides his hand-crafted white cedar canoe across the rippling waters of Eel Lake near Lakeside.

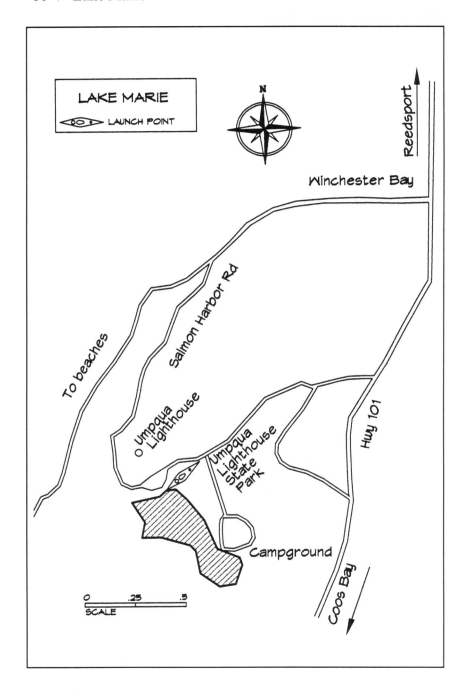

Lake Marie

Location: Within Umpqua Lighthouse State Park, 18 miles north of the Coos Bay Area. (6 miles south of Reedsport.)

Directions: From north end of McCullough Bridge, follow US 101 north 16 miles and turn west on Umpqua Lighthouse Rd. Follow signs to lighthouse. Lake Marie is 0.25 mile west of state park campground.

Facilities/Etc: Restrooms, picnic area, swimming beach, campground, lighthouse, museum.

Launch Site: Sandy beach.

Length: 1 mile

Time: 1 hour

Precautions: Stumps and limbs.

Discussion: Pretty little lake in forested setting. Part of Umpqua Lighthouse State Park, this lake offers easy paddling and is good for families and first-time paddlers.

Eel Lake

Location: Within William Tugman State Park, 1 mile north of Lakeside.

Directions: From north end of McCullough Bridge, follow US 101 11.8 miles and turn east on access road to Tugman State Park. Follow road to parking area at lake's edge.

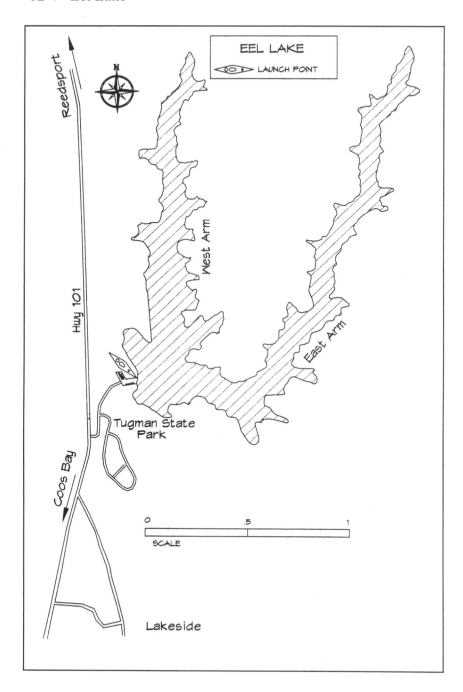

Facilities/Etc: Restrooms, showers, picnic area, fishing dock, campground.

Launch Site: Public boat ramp or adjacent sandy area.

Length/Time: see below

Precautions: Watch for fallen trees along shoreline. North wind can be a factor, especially during summer afternoons.

Discussion: A large, horseshoe-shaped lake surrounded by thick, mostly second-growth forest, Eel Lake has a 5 mph motorboat speed limit (and thus few motorboaters), so it's a great place for a quiet paddle. Bounded on the west end by Tugman State Park, and with much of the rest of its shoreline and upland slopes owned by the Oregon Dept. of Fish and Wildlife, Eel Lake remains pristine, with no housing or other development. There's fishing for stocked rainbow trout, native cutthroat trout and bass. There are many quiet coves, and osprey, ducks and other birds and waterfowl abound. The 355-acre lake is divided into two arms, which conveniently enough "split" in the area directly in front of the boat launch.

West Arm: There's an interesting area at the upper end, where the remains of old logging trestles cut the corner of the lake. A nice wetland can be paddled depending upon lake level.

Length: 2.8 miles round trip
Time: 1+ hour

East Arm: Many small coves offer interesting detours, and some have places to pull into and get out. A hiking/mountain bike trail follows part of the south shore, with overlooks and informal landings.

Length:5.2 miles
Time: 2+ hours

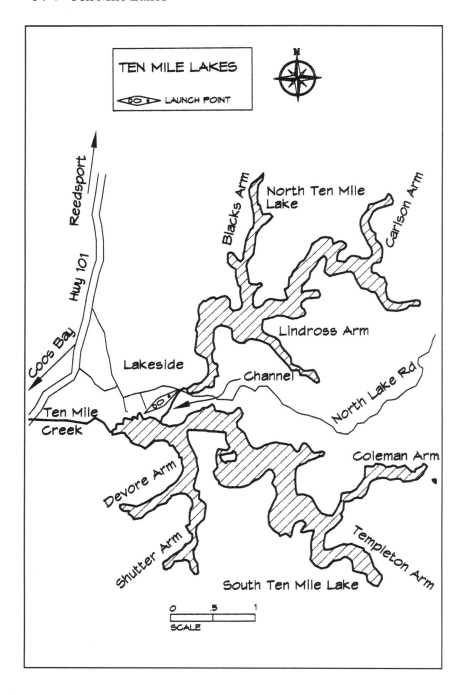

Ten Mile Lakes

Location: About 12 miles north of the Coos Bay Area.

Directions: From north end of McCullough Bridge, follow US 101 north 10.3 miles and turn east, following signs to Lakeside, 1 mile. Follow signs into town and from 8th (or "Main") St., turn east on North Lake Rd., following signs to boat ramp.

Facilities/Etc: Restrooms, picnic area, fishing dock.

Launch Site: Ten Mile Lakes County Park Boat Ramp.

Alternate Launch Sites: There's a concrete boat ramp at the south end of 8th (or "Main") St., to the right just past Hilltop Drive. This launch places you into Ten Mile Creek just downstream from the lake. Another boat ramp into Ten Mile Creek is located on Park Avenue two blocks west of 8th St.

Length: North Ten Mile Lake: 16 miles (19.3)
South Ten Mile Lake: 20 miles (23 miles).

Time: Varying depending on your sense of exploration.

Precautions: Boat wakes. Speeding boats, personal watercraft, waterskiers, anglers, swimmers and racing sailboats.

Discussion: Ten Mile Lakes are actually two lakes, connected by a channel, offering an impressive surface area of 2,727 acres (that's more than 42 miles of shoreline). Said to be the second most-popular recreational lake in the state of Oregon, Ten Mile Lakes are certainly the busiest and most developed of the many freshwater lakes in Dunes Country between the Coos Bay Area and Florence. The lakes are popular with anglers, water skiers, personal watercraft operators

A sandy beach at Ten Mile Lakes County Park offers an excellent put-in place. There are also boat ramps and docks.

and pleasure boaters. On summer weekends, expect a lot of boat wakes and high-speed traffic; there's much less activity on weekdays and in the off-season.

Much of the shoreline is private property, so landing is pretty much limited to the public boat ramp, a couple of private marinas, and some spots at the distant arms of each lake.

At the far end of North Lake, you might find a few places to land under the train trestle in Black's Arm. Other North Lake spots to get out of your boat include the ends of Carlson Arm and Big Arm.

At the eastern reaches of South Lake, there's a sandy beach at the end of Coleman Arm, while the nearby Templeton Arm can sometimes offer places to land where Johnson Creek flows into the lake.

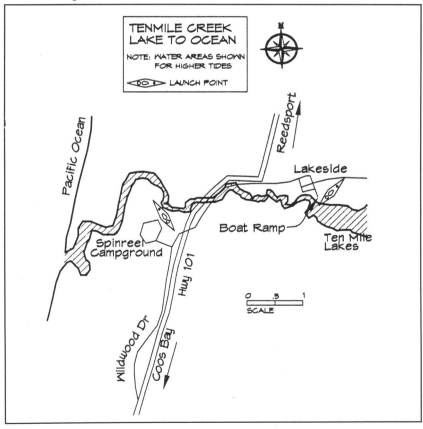

Ten Mile Creek passes through a wide mix of terrain and scenery.
It flows from Ten Mile Lakes through peaceful forests and tall,
jungly brush and grasses . . .

Ten Mile Creek

Location/Directions/Facilities/Launch sites: See previous tour.

Alternate launch site: Spinreel Campground. From north end of
McCullough Bridge, follow US 101 north for 9 miles and take exit for
Sprinreel Campground. Boat ramp is adjacent to parking area
beyond campground. Day-use fee.

Length: 6 miles (Lakeside County Park Boat Ramp to Pacific
Ocean) Spinreel Campground to Pacific Ocean: 3 miles

Time: 3+ hours (entire tour round trip)

Precautions: Ten Mile Creek can have a deceptively strong current.
Watch for submerged trees, limbs, and roots. Use caution around the

. . to the shifting sands and open expanses of the Oregon Dunes. Downriver from Spinreel Campground is this view of a "tree island," a remnant of forest completely surrounded by dunes.

railroad bridge as there are many cut-off pilings. Downed trees and brush may completely block channel at times. Watch for debris. North wind can be strong in summertime from Spinreel Campground to the Pacific Ocean. Use caution around river mouth and ocean. The creek level can raise 2 to 4+ feet during times of high water.

Discussion: This paddle offers quite a challenge if you do the whole trek out and back from Ten Mile Lake, but you can cut the mileage in about half with a put-in at Spinreel Campground, farther down the creek. The whole trip offers one of the most interesting paddles in the region, mainly because the terrain changes so much. You start in the forests around Ten Mile Lake and slowly make a transition to dunes country, and finally to the seashore.

Starting from the beach in Ten Mile County Park in Lakeside, paddle west 0.3 mile to the creek's outlet. The creek passes between marinas and shoreside homes, and goes by two other boat ramps. It weaves through willows, tall brush and trees, then flows under the railroad and US 101 bridges, respectively. It meanders past more homes, and 3 miles downstream from the lake, passes Spinreel Campground. The channel swings north, where you may encounter strong winds head-on in the summer. The creek turns west, sliding through beautiful open dunes, then — surprise! — turns *south* for over 1 mile. The dunes to the north are closed to vehicles, while to the south you may hear and see all-terrain rigs. There are many sandbars and shallow places to stop and get out.

The river turns west, then northwest, and becomes very shallow as it nears the ocean, and you may have to carefully pick your route to avoid getting beached. Low river levels in summer may require you to drag your boat across sandy areas. Don't damage your boat!

Depending on river levels, tide conditions, the wind and your ambition, it's sometimes possible to paddle all the way into the ocean.

Open sand areas near the mouth may be closed to entry by foot March 15 to September 15 to protect the western snowy plover.

Saunders Lake

Location: About 10 miles north of the Coos Bay Area.

Directions: From the north end of McCullough Bridge, follow US 101 north for 6.5 miles and turn northwest on Wildwood Drive, following sign to boat ramp.

Facilities/Etc: Restrooms, picnic area.

Launch Site: Sen. Jack Ripper County Park Boat Ramp or adjacent grassy area to left of ramp. Also off lawns in front of picnic area.

Length: 3 miles (4.1 miles)

Time: 2+ hours

Precautions: Many submerged tree stumps hide in the lake's north end. They may or may not be break the surface — it depends on how much water is in the lake — so watch for them!

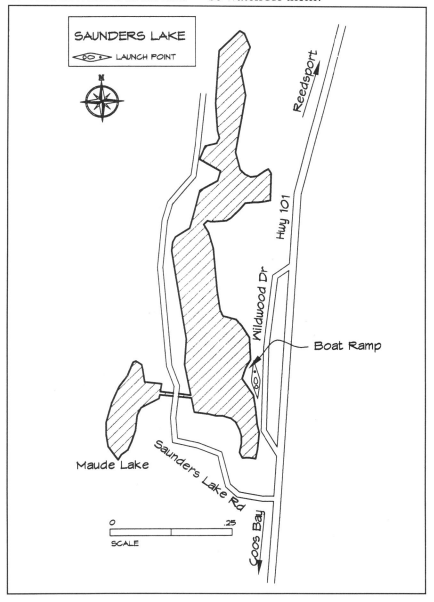

Grassy embankment just below the picnic area is a good place to launch a Saunders Lake expedition. There's also a boat ramp.

Discussion: This is another pretty lake in Dunes Country, with many shoreline homes and some interesting wetlands. From the boat launch, paddle around the bit of land on the left and go under the railroad bridge. From there, paddle along the lake's edge counter-clockwise. There are many coves to explore. At the north end, it becomes shallow, and you can explore the wetlands area. In times of high water, Saunders Lake's overflow spills northward into Clear Lake. Continuing south in Saunders Lake, you can paddle under another vehicle bridge and check out little Maude Lake to the west, then return to Saunders Lake and continue counter-clockwise back to the boat launch.

Beale Lake

Location: Approximately 5 miles north of North Bend in the Oregon Dunes.

Directions: From the north end of McCullough Bridge, go north on US 101 about 4 miles and turn west on Hauser Depot Rd.. Follow it to a "T" intersection at the railroad tracks. Turn north and follow the road about 0.5 mi. The road turns to gravel and crosses the railroad tracks. Bear right once across the tracks, and right again, following the road to the edge of Beale Lake.

Facilities/Etc: None. Very limited parking.

Launch Site: An improvised boat launch has been cleared at the end of the road at water's edge.

Length: 3 miles around perimeter

Time: 2 hours

Precautions: Strong north winds most summer afternoons can make paddling difficult. As the lake levels lower throughout the summer, more weeds will appear at or near the surface.

Discussion: This secluded lake amidst the Oregon Dunes is ideal for easy paddling and picnicking. It's actually three long, narrow lakes connected by small channels, which are easily found. Near the west and north parts of the lakes are sand dunes and sandy beaches. A few small islands invite exploration.

Lily pads dot the surface as kayakers make their way across Beale Lake in the Oregon Dunes north of the Coos Bay Area.

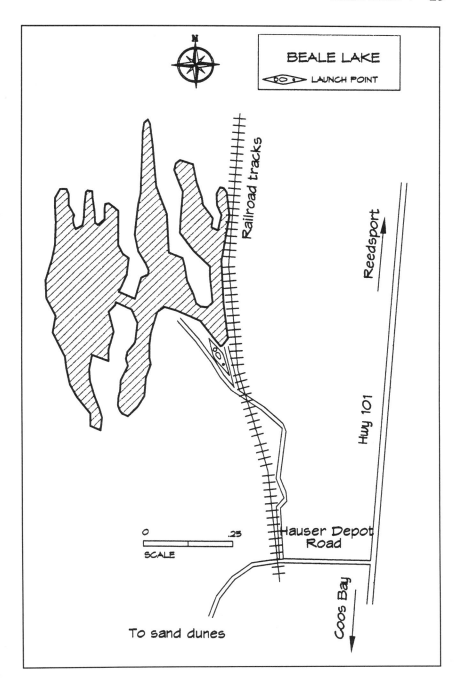

Coos Bay Area

What's variously called Coos Bay, Coos River, or the Coos Bay shipping channel is actually a vast estuary, fed by more than 30 tributaries and covering over 19 square miles of surface area at high tide.

The common denominator throughout the system is the tide. Its reach extends a remarkable *34 miles* up the two main tributaries, the Coos and Millicoma Rivers.

The biggest potential problem with sometimes-drastic tides is the danger of getting stranded on mudflats. The mud is soft, sticky and no fun to slog through! You've got to maintain a sense for the main channel, which is usually identified with standard navigational markers.

The good news is that you can also use the tides to your advantage. By planning trips with the changing tides, you can paddle with the current coming *and* going. Downhill all the way! Or, with a vehicle shuttle, plan more ambitious one-way trips, again utilizing incoming or outgoing tides.

You should obtain a tidebook (available at many local stores) and use the corrections, if any, for the places where you're paddling. Local newspapers also daily print tide charts.

When the term "high tide" is used for these tours, it refers to the time of high tide at the Coos Bay channel entrance/ocean beaches. As you go "upriver," the time of high tide time is later respective to how far upriver you travel. I've tried to note the approximate calculations for determining high tide or low tide, but land observations should always be made prior to paddling. Each trip as described takes advantage of tides and currents.

Wind is also an important influence. There are strong north winds during most summer afternoons. In winter, storms blow in from the south.

The Coos estuary is accessible in literally dozens of places, from official boat ramps and docks, to undeveloped put-ins and beaches. You can make any number of out-and-back trips, or, as suggested earlier, use a vehicle shuttle for longer excursions.

If you're not comfortable "crossing the bay" you can make several interesting expeditions by following the shoreline, or consider launching from one of the sites that offer access to islands in the bay created from dredge materials.

The first tours discuss trips in the main channel, from Charleston "upriver" past Empire, North Bend, Coos Bay, Eastside and up the Coos and Millicoma Rivers.

The later sections deal with the inlets and sloughs of the Coos Bay estuary, including the South Slough National Estuarine Research Reserve.

Approximate tide time corrections for Coos Bay Area:
Empire Boat Ramp: +40 minutes.
Railroad Bridge: +1 hour
North Bend Boat Ramp: +1.10 hour
Downtown Coos Bay: +1.25 hour
Eastside Boat Ramp: +1.35 hour

Charleston to Empire Boat Ramp

Location: About 12 miles southwest of Coos Bay/North Bend.

Directions: From US 101 in North Bend or Coos Bay, follow signs to Charleston, Ocean Beaches, State Parks. The roads eventually lead to Coos Bay's Empire district. Follow the main route (Newmark Ave.) as it heads west toward the edge of the Coos Bay channel. At the foot of Newmark Ave. is the Empire Boat Ramp. The main route to Charleston (Empire Blvd., aka Charleston Hwy) swings south, and follows near the shoreline to Charleston. Cross the bridge over South Slough and turn north on Boat Basin Drive, and continue north to the public boat ramps.

Alternate launch: Just before crossing South Slough Bridge, turn south on Troller Rd. and continue 2 blocks to parking area just before

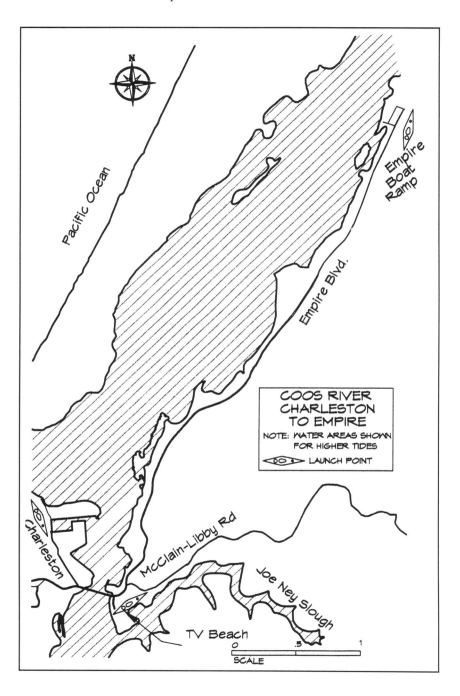

Pacific Ocean

Empire Boat Ramp

Empire Blvd.

COOS RIVER
CHARLESTON
TO EMPIRE
NOTE: WATER AREAS SHOWN
FOR HIGHER TIDES
LAUNCH POINT

Charleston

McClain-Libby Rd

Joe Ney Slough

TV Beach

0   .5   1
SCALE

gates to Port of Coos Bay shipyard. Parking area is marked by sign for Distant Water Fleet Facility. We call it TV Beach because a paddler once noticed a TV set in the mud here, and later removed it for recycling.

Time: 2 hours

Facilities/Etc: Restrooms, showers, full services in Charleston.

Launch Site: Public boat ramps or docks in Charleston marina or from sandy beach at Troller Rd. (TV Beach) launch site.

Length: 3.7 miles one way

Precautions: Watch for swells coming in from channel entrance in vicinity of north and south jetties. Watch for large ships, and fishing and recreational boats. Wind and floating logs can also be a hazard. Water is shallow along eastern shore.

Discussion: Because of wind, ocean swells and the exposed nature of this part of the bay, this isn't among my favorite paddles, but under the right conditions, it can be interesting. It also keeps you on one side of the channel if you're hesitant about crossing the bay.

Launch on an incoming tide from the Charleston docks or boat ramp and swing south out of the harbor. You'll pass Pigeon Point and a small island that is sometimes home to sea lions. Another highlight is the long-abandoned Coos Head sawmill and its old decaying pier.

Empire Boat Ramp to North Spit launch point

Location: 5 miles west of Coos Bay/North Bend.

Directions: From US 101 in North Bend or Coos Bay, follow signs to Charleston, Ocean Beaches, State Parks. The roads eventually lead to Coos Bay's Empire district. Follow the main route (Newmark Ave.) as it heads west toward the edge of the Coos Bay channel. At the foot of Newmark Ave. is Empire Boat Ramp.

Facilities/Etc: Restrooms, picnic tables, boat launch, fishing dock.

Launch Site: Public boat launch or beach area at south end of parking lot.

Length: 2.7 miles

Time: 1+ hour. High tide at Empire is 40 minutes later than time listed in tidebooks for high tide at Coos Bay channel entrance/ocean beaches.

Precautions: This paddle involves a channel crossing. Use caution at all times and do not attempt during storms or heavy chop. Watch for shipping traffic.

Discussion: One of several excursions possible from the Empire Boat Ramp, this tour takes you to a sandy beach over on the North Spit. You could also use this as a jumping-off point to explore islands in the bay, or to continue to other destinations listed in the next tours.

North Spit Boat Ramp Excursions

Location: North Spit of Coos Bay Estuary, about 10 miles west of Coos Bay/North Bend.

Directions: From the north end of McCullough Bridge, continue north on US 101 0.6 mile and turn west on Jordan Cove Rd., following signs to Oregon Dunes, Horsfall Beach. Follow the road across

A row of pilings breaks the wave action near the Bureau of Land Management North Spit Boat Ramp. You can launch several expeditions from here.

the causeway, crossing a bridge and railroad tracks. Continue past the pulp mill to a "Y" intersection, and bear left on Transpacific Parkway, following signs to BLM boat ramp.

Facilities/Etc: Restrooms, picnic tables.

Launch Site: Boat ramp or sandy beach.

Length: Trek described below is 6 miles roundtrip.

Time: 3+ hours, with time for land-based exploration.

Precautions: Use caution when entering bay waters and do not launch during storms or heavy chop. Watch for shipping traffic and boats.

Discussion: You can use the BLM North Spit Boat Ramp as a jumping-off point for several excursions in the bay. Use the tides to your advantage. Visit dredge spoils islands or just cruise along the coves and small inlets. Another fun outing is to launch on the later stages of an outgoing tide, and paddle "downriver" (toward the ocean) on the north side of the channel. Paddle approximately 3 miles until you reach a set of old pilings extending out into the river. These pilings were once used to tie up navel minesweepers. This site is approximately across from the smokestack at the old Coos Head Lumber Co. mill. Beach near the piling and explore the abandoned World War II ammo bunkers and Coast Guard building sites. As you paddle down and back, you will pass several islands that are made from dredge spoils. They make fun exploring. All the area is basically sandy which makes getting on and off land fairly easy.

North Spit launch point to North Bend Boat Ramp

Location: About 3 miles north of North Bend.

Directions: From the north end of McCullough Bridge, continue north on US 101 0.6 mile and turn west on North Spit Causeway, following signs to Oregon Dunes, Horsfall Beach. Drive across the causeway, which crosses a small bridge at its west end. Immediately across the bridge, make a U-turn and park on the south edge of the road. Directly below is a small sandy beach from which you can launch.

Facilities/Etc: none.

Launch Site: Sandy beach.

Length: 2.3 miles one way
Precautions: This paddle requires a channel crossing. Use caution when entering bay waters and do not launch during storms or heavy chop. Watch for shipping traffic.

Discussion: This is yet another potential tour of the lower bay, with highlights that include passage under the swing-span railroad bridge and the soaring green girders of McCullough Bridge. You can also explore Pony Slough (see next tour for more details.) You'll go around the "north bend" that gives the city its name, and pass along part of the working waterfront before arriving at North Bend Boat Ramp.

Pony Slough

Location: On the Coos River channel west of McCullough Bridge and the swing-span railroad bridge. This is the body of water across from Pony Village Mall in North Bend.

Directions: You can launch from the California St. Boat Ramp in North Bend, or from an unimproved shoreline site in North Bend, or from the North Spit launch point across the channel.

North Spit launch point: From the north end of McCullough Bridge, head north on US 101 for 0.6 mile and turn west on Noth Spit Causeway, following signs to Oregon Dunes, Horsfall Beach. Drive across the causeway, which crosses a small bridge at its west end. Immediately across the bridge, make a U-turn and park on the south edge of the road. Directly below is a small sandy beach from which you can launch.

North Bend Boat Ramp: From US 101 northbound or southbound in North Bend, turn east on California St. and follow it to edge of bay.

Alternate Launch Site: For a shorter trip or to avoid paddling around North Point and under McCullough Bridge or across the river, turn off Virginia Ave (west of US 101) onto Monroe Ave. You can go the end of Monroe and launch there or turn onto Florida St. and launch from the end of the street. Launch at or near high tide.

Facilities/Etc: North Bend Boat Ramp has restrooms. No facilities at North Spit or alternate launch sites.

Launch Site: See directions above.

Length: 3 miles depending upon launch site.

Time: 1.5 hours

Discussion: This slough at its end turns into Pony Creek, up which you can paddle a short distance depending on the tide. Paddle only at or near high tide as this area is a mudflat during low tide. The area borders the city of North Bend and the North Bend Airport. If you

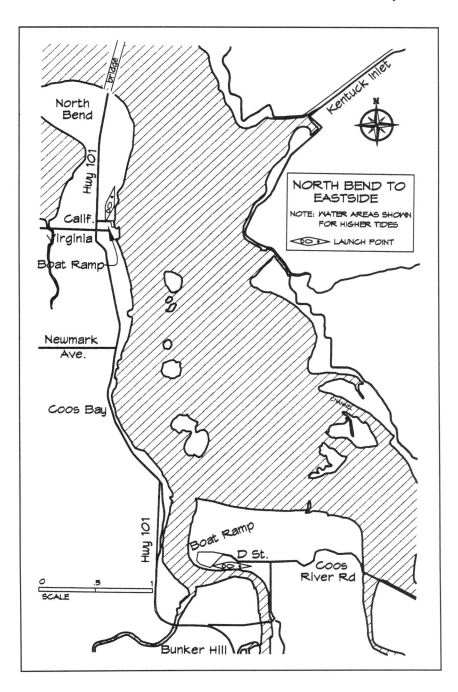

North Bend

Hwy 101

Calif.

Virginia

Boat Ramp

Newmark Ave.

Coos Bay

Hwy 101

Boat Ramp

D St.

Coos River Rd

Bunker Hill

Kentuck Inlet

NORTH BEND TO EASTSIDE

NOTE: WATER AREAS SHOWN FOR HIGHER TIDES

LAUNCH POINT

CHANNEL

0   .5   1
SCALE

are paddling from the North Bend Boat Ramp, paddle north around Simpson Heights, under McCullough Bridge and the railroad bridge. At this point, turn south into the slough. Paddle around the edges watching for shallow areas. Launching from the North Spit launch point will require paddling across the river. The slough is home to many, many birds, and there's a shell-strewn beach adjacent to the railroad bridge's southern approach.

Precautions: Strong north winds can make the slough quite rough. Don't get caught out on a falling tide.

North Bend Boat Ramp to Downtown Coos Bay

Location: Near downtown North Bend, just east of US 101.

Directions: From US 101 in North Bend, turn east on California St. and follow it to the edge of channel.

Facilities/Etc: Restrooms, boat ramp.

Length: 2 miles one way

Crusin' the waterfront, Coos Bay-style.

Time: 1 hour. High tide at North Bend Boat Ramp is 1.10 hour later than time listed in tidebooks for high tide at Coos Bay channel entrance/ocean beaches.

Launch Site: Boat ramp or adjacent shoreline.

Precautions: Be aware of shallow water, and be alert about the tides, as an outgoing tide may strand you in shallow muddy areas. Keep well back from passing commercial boats and ships.

Discussion: You can paddle up the channel to Coos Bay, passing the Mill Casino and other waterfront development, including docks at which ships, barges and tugs are moored. Paddle along the Coos Bay Boardwalk and the public docks. (You can potentially stop at the docks, but they're somewhat high out of the water, making it difficult to get in and out of your craft).

From North Bend Boat Ramp you can also launch trips to the east side of the bay (1.6 mile one-way to Kentuck Inlet), or to the islands in the bay. Or, paddle down-channel to McCullough Bridge, Pony Slough, and other destinations.

Downtown Coos Bay to Eastside

Location: Downtown Coos Bay

Directions: Follow US 101 to downtown Coos Bay. The Coos Bay Boardwalk is parallel to northbound US 101 (Bayshore Drive), with the main entrance at the foot of Anderson St.

Facilities/Etc: Restrooms at Bay Area Chamber of Commerce office. Restrooms at Eastside Boat Ramp.

Launch Site: Public boat dock.

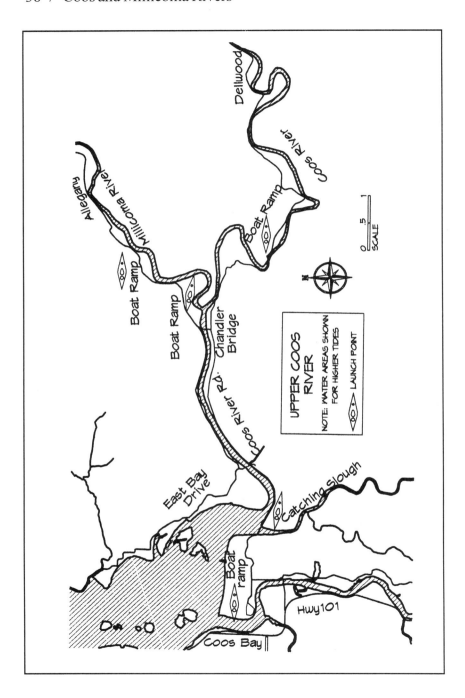

Length: 1 mile

Time: 1 hour. High tide at Coos Bay docks is 1.25 hours later than time listed in tidebooks for high tide at Coos Bay channel entrance/ocean beaches.

Precautions: Watch for fishing, shipping and recreational boats. Wind and floating logs can also be a hazard.

Discussion: This is a potential launch; however, it has a couple of problems: first, you'll have to carry your boat from your vehicle across railroad tracks, go up some stairs, over the docks and down a narrow gangplank. Secondly, the docks are quite high off the water, which makes it difficult to get in and out of your craft. From here you can paddle over to the Eastside boat ramp, or to other destinations discussed in the previous and upcoming tours.

Eastside Boat Ramp to Coos and Millicoma River Landings

Location: Eastside boat ramp is approximately 1 mile east (by land) of Coos Bay; other boat ramps are a various locations upriver (east).

Directions:
Eastside Boat Ramp: From US 101 at the south end of Coos Bay, follow signs to Allegany. Cross Isthmus Slough Bridge and bear left on 6th Ave, following it north 0.5 mile to "T" intersection with D St. Turn west on D St. and follow it to Eastside Boat Ramp.
Doris Place Boat Ramp (Millicoma River): Follow directions above to "T" intersection in Eastside. Turn east on Coos River Rd. and follow it 2.3 miles to Chandler Bridge. Cross bridge, following signs to Allegany. Watch for signs to boat ramp 1.7 miles after crossing bridge.

The Riverside Tavern's private dock is a potential stop along the beautiful Millicoma River.

Rooke-Higgins County Park Boat Ramp (Millicoma River): Follow directions above to Doris Place Boat Ramp and continue upriver 6.2 miles from Chandler Bridge.

Myrtle Tree Boat Ramp (Coos River): Follow directions above to "T" intersection in Eastside. Turn east on Coos River Rd. and follow it 2.3 miles to Chandler Bridge. Do not cross bridge; continue on south bank road, following signs to Coos River Learning Center, Dellwood. Watch for boat ramp 4.5 miles upriver from Chandler Bridge.

Facilities/Etc: Restrooms at all boat ramps. Picnicking and camping at Rooke-Higgins.

Launch Site: See directions above. Launch from boat ramps.

Length: Eastside Boat Ramp to Coos Bay waterfront: 0.4 mile
" " " to Catching Slough Br: 3.1 miles
" " " to forks of rivers: 7.7 miles
" " " to Doris Place Boat Ramp (Millicoma River): 7.8 miles
" " " to Rooke-Higgins County Park Boat Ramp (Millicoma River): 11.2 miles

Eastside Boat Ramp   to Riverside Tavern: 13.1 miles
"   "   "   to Allegany/West Fork (approximate head of tidewater): 16.1 miles
"   "   "   to Myrtle Tree Boat Ramp (Coos River): 10.1 miles
"   "   "   to Dellwood (approximate head of tidewater): 18 miles

Time: Varies depending on length of trip, currents and tide. High tide at Eastside Boat Ramp is 1.35 hours later than time listed in tidebooks for high tide at Coos Bay channel entrance/ocean beaches.

Precautions: The stretch of water from Eastside boat ramp past Catching Slough Bridge is the most exposed of the route. Strong northerly winds can build up adverse wave conditions in the afternoons during the summer and fall seasons.

Discussion: The upper reaches of the Coos and Millicoma Rivers are quite beautiful, although much of the riverside is private property, with few places except public boat ramps to launch or get out. The very nature of these rivers yields few sand bars, gravel bars or easy places to land. You can, however, use the tides for easy out-and-back tours from the various launching points. *Note that in summer and the fall, tidal influences will overcome the river current and cause the current to run upstream on an incoming tide. During the winter and spring after long periods of rainfall, the river current will prevail over tidal influences.*

No trip up the Millicoma River is complete without a stop at the docks below the Riverside Tavern. The setting is quite pretty and there are picnic tables you're welcome to use. The folks who run the tavern and café are friendly — even if you don't buy a beer it's a nice idea to say hey!

Coos Bay Area Inlets and Sloughs

As discussed in the previous section on the Coos Bay Area, the vast Coos estuary includes more than three dozen tidal arms, many of which offer excellent paddling. One of them, the South Slough National Estuarine Research Reserve, has the distinction of being the nation's first such preserve, while others are also protected from development.

The tidal arms are often – and quite correctly – called sloughs, although early-day community boosters preferred the term *inlet*, thinking the word "slough" too dismal and swampy-sounding.

Thus the seeming-contradiction at times over such place names as Pony *Slough* and Haynes *Inlet*.

North Slough (Hauser Channel)

Location: 1 mile north of McCullough Bridge.

Directions: From McCullough Bridge, head north on US 101 for 0.6 mile and turn west on North Spit Causeway, following signs to Oregon Dunes and Horsfall Beach. Drive across the causeway, which crosses a small bridge at its west end. Immediately across the bridge, make a U-turn and park on the south edge of the road. Directly below is a small sandy beach from which you can launch. This launch site can also be used for paddling Haynes Inlet or into the Coos Bay channel.

Facilities/Etc: none.

Launch Site: Small sandy beach.

Length: 7.1 miles round trip

Time: 3+ hours

Precautions: Submerged pilings. Pay close attention to tides and beware of being stranded on a falling tide.

Discussion: Great wetlands paddle. Many birds including eagles, egrets, and herons can be observed. Begin your paddle at approximately the time listed in tide charts for high tide at the Coos Bay channel entrance/ocean beaches, and you will have the incoming tide with you. (See page 7 for important notes about tide times.)

Paddle under the vehicle bridge adjacent to the put-in beach and head north. You can stay to the west edge of the slough as you go north, paddling over shallow water. Continue north. The waterway will narrow. Once past the narrowed section, begin to head east toward US 101. The main channel parallels US 101. You can explore the wetlands away from the channel *but beware of being caught out on a falling tide*. Continue to paddle north until you come to the bridge and tidegate under US 101. Turn around and paddle back at this point. (You could also take out here if you wish, but do so only if it's high tide; the steep embankment makes access difficult during low tide.) If you have timed your trip correctly, the tide will have changed just as you reach the turn-around point, and you'll have the outgoing current with you on the return trip.

Haynes Inlet

Location/Directions/Launch site/Facilities: See previous tour.

Alternate launch site: 0.2 mi north of McCullough Bridge on US 101, turn east on North Bay Drive and continue approximately 1 mile to a county boat ramp just before the Claussen Oyster plant. Follow information in previous chapter on North Slough for location, directions and launch site.

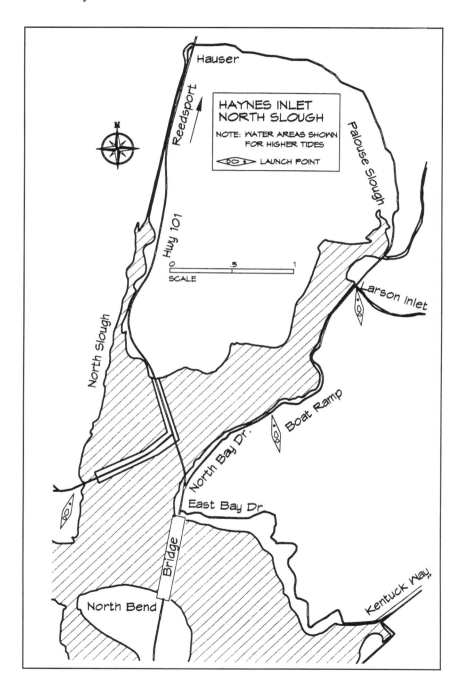

HAYNES INLET
NORTH SLOUGH

NOTE: WATER AREAS SHOWN
FOR HIGHER TIDES

LAUNCH POINT

Length: 8 miles if you paddle the perimeter of the inlet.

Time: Approximately 3 hours depending on how much exploring you do.

Precautions: All of this paddle is within a part of the bay greatly influenced by tides, with shallow water and mudflats on the margins. Paddling on the incoming tide should allow you to safely travel the area. Various navigational signs mark the main channel. Strong wind can be focused around the Haynes Inlet bridge. Also watch for oyster harvesting and fishing boats. By the way, all oyster beds are private property, so no poaching!

Discussion: Beautiful backwaters of the bay, rich with wildlife and birds. Launch at the time listed in tide charts for high tide at the Coos Bay channel entrance/ocean beaches. (See important note about tides on page 7.) If possible, paddle in the morning when winds are likely to be at a minimum. Paddle west, parallel to the causeway, toward US 101 and Haynes Inlet Bridge. Paddle under the bridge. The current will be strongest here, due to the narrowing of the inlet. If the expected tide is reasonably high, you can turn left after paddling under the bridge and explore this part of the slough. Paddle north, parallel to US 101, until you reach the northern shore, then follow the shoreline east.

At the extreme eastern end of Haynes Inlet is Palouse Creek. Depending upon tide height, you can paddle up this creek, which is all tidelands. Many birds will be found in this area. After paddling the creek and returning to Haynes Inlet, continue to paddle clockwise, eventually circling back toward the west to your starting point.

Along the way you'll pass Lone Rock, a small, picturesque island. North Bay Drive runs along the shoreline here, and you might also notice a public boat ramp near an oyster processing plant. Depending upon tide heights, you'll also see a couple of small sandy beaching areas if you want to get out of your boat.

Larson Inlet

Location: About 2 miles from North Bend.

Directions: From McCullough Bridge, follow US 101 north about 0.2 mile, and turn east on North Bay Drive. Drive approximately 2.5 miles up North Bay Drive and turn south on Larson Way.

Facilities/Etc: none.

Launch Site: Right next to the bridge/tidegate at the intersection of Larson Way and North Bay Drive.

Length: 5 miles if the tide is quite high, or if heavy rainfall has recently occurred.

Time: 2 hours.

Precautions: Shallow water. Beware of being caught on an outgoing tide.

Discussion: Very narrow winding paddle through a small valley. Peaceful countryside, with cattle ranches lining the route and lots of birdlife in residence. The channel narrows into shallow, reedy wetlands.

Launch 1.5 hours before time listed in tide charts for high tide at the Coos Bay channel entrance/ocean beaches. (See important note about tides on page 7.) You will have the incoming tide with you as you head upchannel, and an outgoing tide for your return.

SOUTH SLOUGH AREA

The southern arms of the Coos Bay estuary near Charleston include Jo Ney Slough and the Winchester and Sengstacken inlets of South Slough National Estuarine Research Reserve. You can start expeditions in several places. Launch out-and-back trips from Charleston, exploring the inlets and shoreline, and visit Valino Island, a 23-acre island within the research reserve. Or launch out-and-back paddles from the Hinch Rd. put-in within South Slough Reserve. Best of all is to plan a shuttle, leaving a vehicle at either end.

Wherever you paddle in South Slough, be sure to account for the tides. Don't be caught out in the mud on a falling tide!

South Slough National Estuarine Research Reserve

Location: About 12 miles west of Coos Bay/North Bend.

Directions: From US 101 in North Bend or Coos Bay, follow signs to Ocean Beaches, State Parks, Charleston. You'll eventually end up in Coos Bay's Empire District, on Newmark Ave. Follow Newmark to the edge of the bay, and then swing south as the road becomes Empire Blvd. (aka Charleston Highway and Cape Arago Highway). Once in Charleston, there are two potential put-ins.

Troller Rd. put-in (TV Beach): Just before crossing South Slough Bridge, turn south on Troller Rd. and follow it several blocks to a parking area just before the gates to the Port of Coos Bay shipyards. A sign identifies this as the Distant Water Fleet Facility. We call it TV Beach because a paddler once noticed an old TV stuck in the mud here. For the sake of the environment, he later hauled it off.

Charleston Harbor Boat Ramp: Follow directions above, and

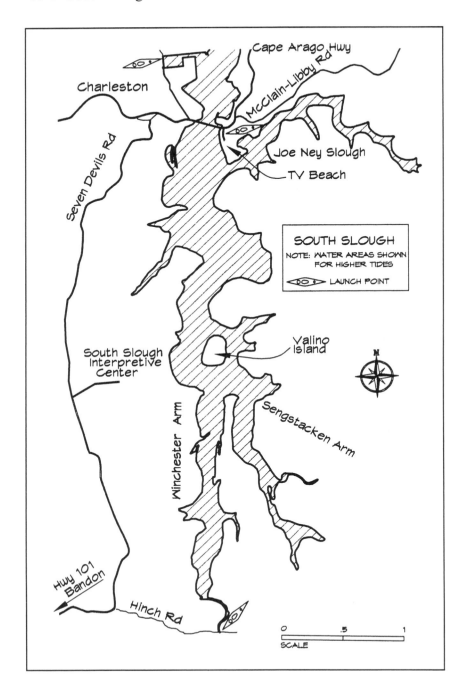

cross the South Slough Bridge in Charleston. One block past the bridge turn north on Boat Basin Way and follow signs to boat ramp.

Hinch Rd. put-in: Follow directions above and proceed over South Slough bridge and through Charleston. Just beyond Charleston turn south on Seven Devils Rd., and follow it 5.3 miles to Hinch Rd., marked by a sign that says South Slough National Estuarine Research Reserve. Follow gravel Hinch Rd. to the edge of the slough.

Facilities/Etc: Restrooms and showers are available near boat ramp in Charleston. Restrooms and showers are available in the Port of Coos Bay shipyard on Troller Rd.. No facilities at Hinch Rd. put-in.

Launch sites: See directions above.

Length: Troller Rd. put-in to Hinch Rd. take-out: 4+ miles one-way if you take a direct route; longer if you paddle all the shoreline.

Time: 2.5 hours minimum. Longer if you explore all the available area.

Precautions: Watch for shallow areas. In the summer, the north wind can be quite strong resulting in very rough water conditions particularly when combined with strong tides. Plan your trip early in the morning if possible. Winter storms will bring strong winds from the south. The first part of the paddle is more exposed than the last half of the trip.

Discussion: Established in 1975 as the nation's first estuarine reserve, the South Slough National Estuarine Research Reserve is comprised of 4,700 acres, 700 of which are tidelands and freshwater marshes. The reserve also features a 23-acre island. Birdlife is abundant, and this is one of the premier paddles in the region. The South Slough Reserve's interpretive center (PO Box 5417, Charleston OR 97420, 541-888-5558) has a comprehensive paddling

Kayaker Kate Fieland is happy to reach the Hinch Road take-out in the South Slough National Estuarine Research Reserve.

brochure, and also has frequent guided paddle tours in the summer.

It's best to paddle on an incoming tide. The usual tour is to paddle from Charleston to the Hinch Rd. take-out. This will require a vehicle shuttle; park one at the Hinch Rd. site and return to launch from the beach at Charleston.

Valino Island is located about 2.2 miles from the Charleston launch site. This island had early settlers' homes, even a casino and saloon in 1910. A little south of Valino Island, stay to the west and paddle into Winchester Arm.

It's easy to paddle into dead-end areas, so be prepared to turn around and paddle back out and into the main channel!

Sengstacken Arm: If you paddle to the east from Valino Island, you'll enter Sengstacken Arm, which has no-take out area to allow for a vehicle shuttle, but is perhaps the best and most interesting part of South Slough. Begin this paddle from the Troller Rd. put-in, about 1.5 hours before high tide. Paddle south toward Valino Island. If it is building to a fairly high tide, you can paddle around the east side of the island. The deepest part of the channel is toward the eastern shore. Otherwise, paddle around the island on its west side. (approximately 2 miles from the Troller Rd. put-in).

After rounding the island, paddle toward the east and into Sengstacken Arm. Continue south. Paddling to the extreme end will bring you the junction of Johns's Creek (3.3 miles from Troller Rd. put-in) and Talbot Creek. If it is a fairly high tide, you may be able to paddle up John's Creek for some distance. It narrows to a channel of about 15 to 20 feet. The distance to this point from the put-in is 3.8 miles. At the junction, paddling east will take you up Talbot Creek for approximately 0.5 mile depending upon tide heights. The most interesting side trip would be to paddle through the notch into Elliott Creek. Once through the notch, the creek widens into another small bay. The channel is to the right. Paddling to the end will bring you to a tidegate. Paddling all the creeks and returning to the Troller Rd. put-in would give you a total distance of approximately 10 miles.

Precautions: Strong north winds could make paddling back to your starting point difficult. Be sure to consult your tide table and paddle only on an incoming tide. Getting caught out on a falling tide will result in being stuck in the mud.

Hinch Rd. put-in/take-out: In addition to putting in or taking out for a trip through the main part of South Slough, you can also paddle further south by going under the vehicle bridge here. It's possible to paddle approximately another 1 mile depending upon tide height. The channel is narrow, winding and very interesting.

Joe Ney Slough

Location/Directions/Facilties/Launch Site: See previous tour and launch from the Troller Rd. (TV Beach) site.

Length: 3.2 miles round trip

Time: 2+ hours

Precautions: Beware of shallow areas on an outgoing tide. These shallow areas are basically mudflats. Do not disturb commercial oyster beds.

Discussion: This is a winding, mellow paddle in protected waters. From the Troller Rd. (TV Beach) launch site, paddle south and turn left around the boat yard into Joe Ney Slough. Going right takes you into the South Slough area. Many birds are present, and you also paddle through private oyster beds. The tour ends at an earthen dam that impounds water in a reservoir for the Coos Bay Area's water system. There's an interesting fish ladder. If you launch just before high tide, you will be able to use the current to your advantage plus you will be able to explore a larger area.

Coalbank Slough

Location: South end of Coos Bay.

Directions: From south end of Coos Bay on US 101, follow sign to Allegany. Cross Isthmus Slough Bridge and bear left on 6th Ave, following it north 0.5 mile to "T"intersection with D St. Turn west on D St. and follow it to Eastside Boat Ramp. See map on page 54.

Facilities/Etc: Restrooms.

Launch Site: Launch from boat ramp or dock.

Alternate launch site: Directly below the US 101 bridge over Coalbank Slough, you can launch from a sandy beach. Roads from the bridge's east end lead to the beach.
Alternate launch site: Two blocks east of US 101 bridge over Coalbank Slough, turn south on Harriet St. In 2 blocks turn west on Empire Ave., which becomes McCallum St. in about 2 blocks, then changes name again to Coalbank Ave. Pass TV studios and continue to intersection with Broadway Ave. Boat ramp is along waterway near "Dead End" sign.

Length: 5 miles paddling from the Eastside Boat Ramp.

Time: 2 hours. High tide at the entrance to Coalbank Slough is about 1.5 hours later than high tide at Charleston/ocean beaches.

Precautions: Use caution crossing the bay and do not launch during storms or heavy chop. Watch for shipping traffic.

Discussion: This slough wanders southwest through Coos Bay's Englewood district, ending in the Libby area. Parts of the channel remain in a wild, undeveloped condition, while other sections are lined

Flowing from the working waterfront to a residential district,
Coalbank Slough has remarkably peaceful stretches, too.

with industrial development and homes, some with funky, interesting back yards. This channel leads to canyons once mined for coal, hence the name. At high tide, there's a lot of shallow-water paddling, and you can explore the tidelands. Watch for nesting waterfowl right along the waterside. The channel ends at a dike.

Catching Slough

Location: Approximately 5 miles east of the city of Coos Bay.

Directions: From the south end of Coos Bay on US 101, follow signs to Allegany. The road crosses Isthmus Slough Bridge, and veers north following signs to Allegany, Catching Slough. Continue north 1 mile to a "T" intersection and turn east, following signs to Allegany and Catching Slough. In 1.1 miles the road crosses Catching Slough Bridge. Just across the bridge, turn south on Catching Slough Rd. and park in area below bridge. See map on page 38.

Facilities/Etc: none

Launch Site: Level embankment below east end of bridge.

Length: 8+ mile round trip.

Time: 3+ hours.

Precautions: Debris, limbs and other floating items especially after heavy rains. Beware of being caught on mudflats on outgoing tide.

Discussion: Winding paddle through farmland and wooded areas. Consider the tide when launching. If you plan to paddle to the end and back, try to start about 2 hours before the time listed in tide charts for high tide at the Coos Bay channel entrance/ocean beaches, and use the incoming current to take you up the slough.

Few places in the Coos Bay Area so dramatically illustrate the effects of tidal extremes as Catching Slough. These photos, taken at the eastern end of Catching Slough Bridge at typical high and low tides, show what a difference a few hours make.

At high tide (photo this page), water laps right to the edge of an unimproved boat ramp, but at low tide (photo on opposite page),the channel is several hundred feet away -- through sticky mud. If you paddle in these sloughs, stay in the main channel!

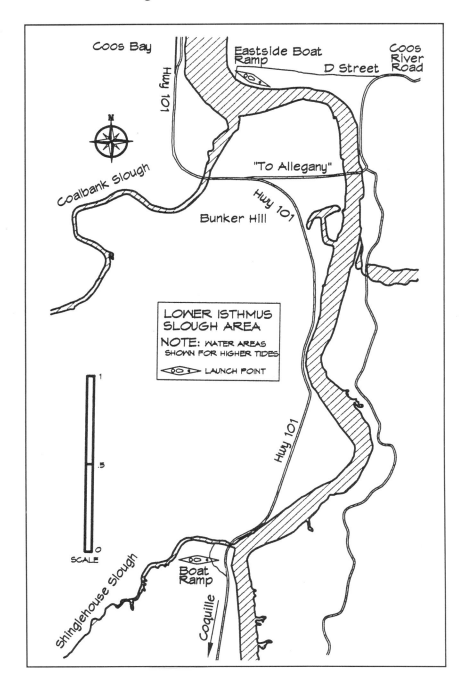

Coos Bay

Hwy 101

Eastside Boat Ramp

D Street

Coos River Road

Coalbank Slough

"To Allegany"

Hwy 101

Bunker Hill

LOWER ISTHMUS SLOUGH AREA

NOTE: WATER AREAS SHOWN FOR HIGHER TIDES

LAUNCH POINT

Hwy 101

1

.5

0

SCALE

Shinglehouse Slough

Boat Ramp

Coquille

ISTHMUS SLOUGH

Isthmus Slough reaches out from the south end of Coos Bay, weaving its way for about 10 miles and branching out into a couple of interesting little side-sloughs before ending at a tidegate near the settlement of Greenacres. It was an important pioneer waterway, and fascinating, crumbling remnants of that era remain to this day, visible only from the water.

You can access Isthmus Slough from Coos Bay's main channel, or begin your explorations at boat ramps and a put-in along the slough. It's always best to use the tides to your advantage when exploring Isthmus Slough, so be sure to consult your tidebook. I've provided the tide differentials for high tide at each put-in.

Consider a vehicle shuttle if you're planning a full paddle of Isthmus Slough. Also remember that this is a working waterway for the wood industry, so be aware of tugboats, barges and log rafts. Incidentally, log rafts tend to concentrate currents, since they force a narrowing of the channel in places.

Isthmus Slough holds many traces of the Coos region's history. For example, a tiny inlet along the way is the final resting place of an old ferry -- watch for its distinctive "bare bones." At Southport are crumbling old piers and docks, and near Davis Slough you can find the remains of a number of coal barges and other watercraft. Pioneer-era railroads ran over and alongside the sloughs on wood trestles still visible today, while pilings and foundations of old towns can be found on the east side of the slough.

From Isthmus Slough, three sloughs branch off. They are shorter paddles and can easily be done on a round-rip basis. They should all be done at or near high tide.

Eastside Boat Ramp and Isthmus Slough Boat Ramps

Location: Eastside Boat Ramp is about 3 miles east (by land) from downtown Coos Bay. Other Isthmus Slough boat ramps and a put-in are located along US 101 at various points for approximately 10 miles south of Coos Bay.

Directions:

Eastside Boat Ramp: From south end of Coos Bay on US 101, follow sign to Allegany. Cross Isthmus Slough Bridge and bear left on 6th Ave, following it north 0.5 mile to "T" intersection with D St. Turn west on D St. and follow it to Eastside Boat Ramp.

Shinglehouse Slough Boat Ramp: From Coos Bay, go south on US 101 3 miles to Shinglehouse Slough, Just past Shinglehouse Slough Road and US 101 bridge over slough, near milepost 242, turn west into parking area for boat ramp.

Davis Slough launch site: From south end of Coos Bay, go south on US 101 approximately 4.5 miles to "Y" junction of US 101 and Highway 42, and take Highway 42. Just past bridge over Davis Slough, turn northwest on connector road that leads back to US 101. Launch from grassy area along road.

Greenacres Boat Ramp: From south end of Coos Bay, go south on US 101 approximately 4.5 miles to "Y" junction of US 101 and Highway 42, and take Highway 42 about 3.2 miles (7.7 miles total from Coos Bay) to Greenacres exit. Follow Greenacres Rd. down to and across railroad tracks. Bear left at "Y" intersection and continue about 300 feet and turn into boat ramp parking area.

Facilities/Etc: Restrooms at Eastside Boat Ramp. No facilities at other boat ramps or launch site.

Launch Site: See directions for each site.

Length: Eastside Boat Ramp to Shinglehouse Slough Boat Ramp: 3.1 miles. High tide at Eastside Boat Ramp +1.35 hour.

Shinglehouse Slough Boat Ramp to Davis Slough put-in: 3.2 miles. High tide at Davis Slough +2.30 hours.

Davis Slough put-in to Greenacres Boat Ramp: 2.7 miles. High tide at Greenacres +3 hours.

Precautions: See discussion above.

Shinglehouse Slough

Location: 3 miles south of Coos Bay.

Directions: From south end of Coos Bay, follow US 101 south about 2.1 miles. Pass Singlehouse Slough Rd., cross bridge over slough and turn into parking area near milepost 242.

Facilities/Etc: None

Launch Site: A public boat ramp is located on the southwest side of the highway. From here, you can paddle Shinglehouse Slough or out into Isthmus Slough.

Length: 2 miles round trip

Time: 1 hour. High tide at the entrance of this slough is approximately 2 hours later than the time listed in tide charts for high tide at the Coos Bay channel entrance/ocean beaches.

Precautions: Old wood pilings line one side of the slough and some may be partially submerged.

Discussion: Relatively short paddle. More area is available at high tide. The channel narrows and becomes a shallow, reedy area.

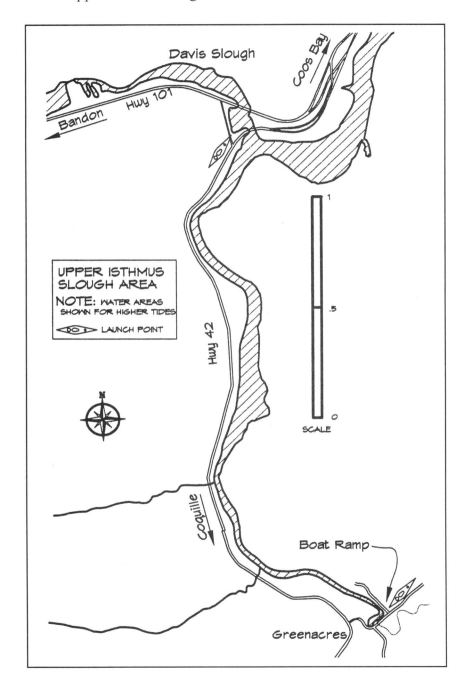

The peaceful, forested backwaters of Davis Slough are among the highlights of a trip along Isthmus Slough south of Coos Bay.

Davis Slough

Location: 5 miles south of Coos Bay at the junction of US 101 and Highway 42.

Directions: From Coos Bay, go south on US 101 4.5 miles to "Y" junction of US 101 and Highway 42, and take Highway 42. Just past bridge over Davis Slough, turn northwest on connector road that leads back to US 101.

Facilities/Etc: None.

Launch Site: Launch only at or near high tide. Launch from the side road that links Highway 42 and US 101. (See map) Here you'll find a triangle of water between two bridges. At high tide, you can launch from a grassy area, but as the tide falls, this will become a fairly steep mud bank.

Length: 2.8 miles

Time: 1+ hour. High tide for this site is approximately 3 hours from the listed high tide.

Precautions: Lots of old pilings. At very high tides, you may not be able to paddle under the bridges.

Discussion: Paddle under US 101 bridge and head west. The slough splits into two parts. The left channel parallels US 101 briefly, and there are sections of old logging train trestles. The left channel ends at a culvert. The right channel opens into a wider wetlands that can be paddled at higher tides, and ends at a diked embankment. The area available to paddle is greatly dependent on the height of the tide. There are parts of logging train trestles along the south side of slough.

COQUILLE RIVER

The Coquille River can be paddled from Bandon to areas above Myrtle Point, when river levels permit. Tidal influences can be felt as far as 30 miles upriver, so be aware of the tides and current. Avoid late summer and fall paddling above the city of Coquille, as the river levels can be quite low. Keep a close eye out for debris in the river that includes trees, limbs and stumps. Remember that most of the riverbank land is private property. Consider a vehicle shuttle if you want to paddle the entire river. You could also paddle various sections of the river, leaving shuttle vehicles at any of the eight boat ramps along the river: Old Town Bandon, Bullards Beach State Park, Rocky Point County Park, Riverton County Park, Sturdivant City Park, Arago County Park and Myrtle Point. Directions to each is provided below.

The most scenic areas are from Bandon to the end of Randolph Island. You might spot harbor seals or river otters in the water, and there are picturesque old hulks of boats and remnants of early-day buildings, piers and townsites along the way. Birds thrive in this estuary, and there's a National Wildlife Refuge not far upriver.

The Moore Mill truck shop sags slowly into the harbor near Old Town Bandon.

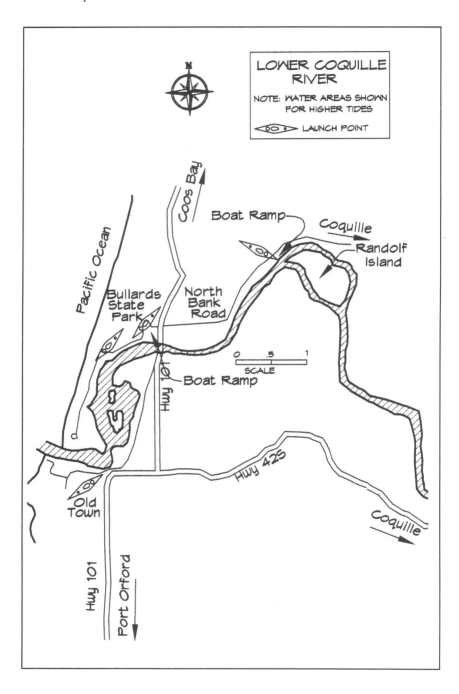

Old Town Bandon to Bullards Beach State Park

Location: Boat harbor in Old Town Bandon

Directions: From US 101 in Bandon, follow signs to Old Town and harbor.

Facilities/Etc: Restrooms, picnic tables, fishing docks at harborside; full services in Bandon; restrooms, day-use and camping at Bullards Beach State Park.

Launch Site: Public docks or boat ramp.

Length: 2 miles one way

Time: 1+ hours

Precautions: Tree stumps, pilings and debris along the shoreline. Also watch for fishing and recreational boats.

Discussion: Among the most scenic sections of the Coquille River, with plentiful birdlife and many interesting sights. Current touring information can be found at Adventure Kayak along the waterfront in Old Town Bandon. From the harbor, cross the river and paddle north along the sandy banks of the river. As the river turns east, the shoreline becomes rocky as it approaches Bullards Beach State Park boat ramp. On a very high tide, you can paddle to the right as you go upriver into the Bandon Marsh National Wildlife Refuge.

Bullards Beach to Rocky Point

Location: 2 miles north of Bandon.

Directions: From stoplight in Bandon at US 101 and Highway 42S, head north on US 101. Cross the Coquille River Bridge, and in 0.5 mile turn west, following signs to Bullards Beach State Park.

Facilities/Etc: Restrooms. State park campground nearby.

Launch Site: Public boat ramp with docks. Docks removed in winter and early spring.
Alternate launch site: Follow road to lighthouse another 0.5 mile beyond boat ramp to a sandy beach alongside road.

Length: 2.5 miles one way

Time: 1+ hours

Discussion: Nice river paddle, directly across from Bandon National Wildlife Refuge, home to wide variety of birds. The tour passes under Coquille River Bridge, and past remnants of Indian fish weirs on north bank. Upriver is Prosper, once a pioneer settlement with mills and fish plants. In later years many of the homes acquired blue metal roofs, and the site was considered for a marina.

Rocky Point County Park and Randolf Island

Location: 1.1 miles upriver from the junction of the North Bank Rd. and US 101.

Directions: Follow US 101 north from Bandon, crossing the Coquille River Bridge. Just past the bridge turn east on North Bank Rd. and continue 1.1 miles to Rocky Point County Park.

Facilities/Etc: Restrooms, picnic tables.

Launch Site: Boat ramp, dock or nearby grassy embankments. Launch about 1 hour before high tide time at mouth of Coquille River/ocean beaches.

Length: 3.1 miles total round trip, around island.

Time: 2 hours. High tide is approximately 30 minutes later than time listed in tide charts for high tide at Bandon/ocean beaches.

Precautions: Submerged or partially-submerged logs and debris in river, especially during or after seasonal rains. Watch for old pilings. Fishing and recreational boats can create wake.

Discussion: The river has split into two channels here as it goes around Randolf Island. Paddle up the "left" (north) side of the river, passing under a couple of old bridges. There's quiet paddling and plentiful birdlife. Harbor seals might also be spotted in the river. Continue around the island and come back downstream to Rocky Point. Paddle at near-high tide as you will be paddling both up and down river.

Rocky Point County Park to Riverton

Location/Directions/Facilities/Launch Site: See previous tour.

Length: 9 miles

Time: 3 hours

Precautions: Watch for floating limbs, branches and debris.

Discussion: This tour passes the site of the pioneer-era settlement of Parkersburg, and includes peaceful stretches where the shoreline roads have cut inland for a few miles.

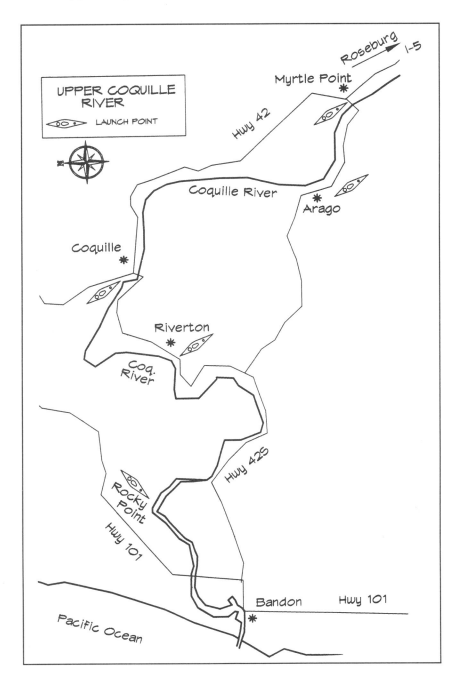

Riverton Boat Ramp to Sturdivant Park

Location: 10 miles east of Bandon.

Directions: From US 101 at Bandon, take Highway 42 S, following signs to Coquille. In about 9.1 miles, turn north into parking area for Riverton County Park Boat Ramp.

Facilities/Etc: Restrooms, picnic tables.

Launch Site: Boat ramp or river bank.

Length: 6.4 miles

Time: 2+ hours depending on tide and current.

Precautions: Watch for debris in river.

Discussion: Peaceful river paddle. Among the sights are three sets of pilings that once supported an early-day coal bunkering facility. The coal came from mines in nearby hills. You'll pass the outlet of Beaver Slough, as well as a water outtake for the Roseburg Lumber Co. mill and Cunningham Creek, just before Sturdivant Park.

Sturdivant Park to Arago Boat Ramp

Location: About 20 miles east of Bandon, near city of Coquille.

Directions: From Bandon, follow Highway 42 S to Coquille. Park is just across bridge over river before Highway 42 S junction with Highway 42 in Coquille.

Facilities/Etc: Restrooms, picnic tables, seasonal camping. Park may be closed due to high water in winter and early spring.

Launch Site: Boat ramp or dock. Dock removed in winter and early spring.

Length: 6.5 miles

Time: 3+ hours depending on current and tide. High tide at Sturdivant Park Boat Ramp is 3 hours later than at river's mouth; 3.45 hours later at Arago boat ramp.

Precautions: Watch for debris in river.

Discussion: Further meanders of the peaceful Coquille River. Sturdivant Park is the site of a historic spruce mill. Just upriver was the original waterfront of Coquille, but not a trace remains. Beyond that is a popular fishing spot called Dutch John Hole. You'll pass the city of Coquille's water outtake pumps, as well as Glen Aiken and Rink Creeks. Johnson Mill Pond and Dement County Fishing Park are along here, although it's hard to spot them from the water and there are few places to disembark. Three more creeks feed into the river along here.

Arago Boat Ramp to Myrtle Point

Location: About 25 miles east of Bandon.

Directions: From Bandon, take Highway 42 S, following signs to Coquille. At intersection of Highway 42 S and Highway 42, turn south, following signs to Roseburg. In about 7 miles, take exit to Arago and follow signs to boat ramp.

Facilities/Etc: Restrooms and picnic tables. Dock is removed in winter and early spring.

Launch Site: Boat ramp or dock (removed in winter).

Time: 2+ hours depending on current and tide. Hide tide at Myrtle Point is 4 hours later than at river's mouth.

Precautions: Watch for debris in water. Current can be strong in winter and spring — not recommended for travel during high water times.

Discussion: Under the right conditions this can be another enjoyable paddle up the meanders of the Coquille River. You'll pass Grady Creek, as well as the confluence with the Coquille River's North Fork before arriving in Myrtle Point. Depending on river levels, it's possible to continue beyond Myrtle Point. (The river splits into its middle and south forks about 4.6 miles up from Myrtle Point.)

Beaver Slough

Location: 10 miles southeast of Coos Bay

Directions: From the south end of Coos Bay, follow US 101 south 4.5 miles to the "Y" intersection with Highway 42, and follow Highway 42 about 6.6 miles (11.1 miles total from Coos Bay) to North Bank Rd. Turn west on North Bank Rd. and cross a bridge over railroad tracks, and another over Beaver Slough. Just past the Beaver Slough bridge, turn north on Old Beaver Hill Rd. Bear right and park in an area just before a "Dead End Road" sign. A path leads down to the slough.

Facilities/Etc: none.

Launch Site: Grassy embankment.

Length: 2.7 miles round trip, paddling to the ends in both directions.

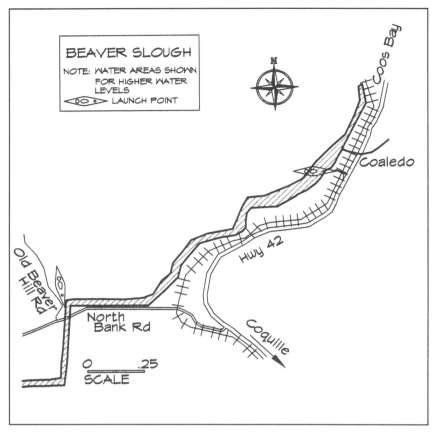

Time: 2 hours or more

Precautions: Narrow winding channel usable mostly during winter and spring during high water. Shorter boats will be easier to paddle here.

Discussion: This slough is an important part of the history of the Coquille Valley area, since it offered the easiest way to move people and goods between the valley and the Coos Bay Area. Small boats and canoes came up Beaver Slough from the Coquille River, then the goods were unloaded and carried over a rise of hills to Isthmus

Slough, an arm of Coos Bay. This part of the trek reminded settlers of crossing the Isthmus of Panama, hence the name Isthmus Slough.

As for the name Beaver Slough, it's easy to see how that was chosen, since evidence of beaver activity abounds to this day. In earlier times, it was a constant challenge to keep the narrow passage clear of dams. Beavers rebuilt their lodges nearly as quickly as they were knocked down. You'll see at least one huge beaver house still standing.

You can paddle in either direction from the put-in, following the slough to its head, or back down nearly to its confluence with the Coquille River (an irrigation pipe blocks passage into the Coquille River.)

Paddling upchannel: Best in times of high water. Parallel railroad tracks and Highway 42, and pass under an old rotten bridge. Farther along is Beaver Creek, which can be paddled for a short distance, passing under Highway 42. Watch out for submerged barbed wire fencing near the bridge. The main channel continues north to its terminus at an embankment.

Paddling down-channel: The slough passes under the North Bank Rd. bridge and flows into a straight channel between pasturelands. Continue paddling until you reach an irrigation pipe, which forces a turn-around at this point. (The slough continues to its meeting with the Coquille River.)

New River

Location: Approximately 15 miles south of Bandon.

Directions: There are three ways to access New River, one of which was still being developed as this book went to press.
Four Mile Rd.: (Completion planned winter of 2002.) From the stoplight in Bandon at US 101 and 11th Ave., go south on US 101 about 7.3 miles and turn west on Lower Four Mile Rd. The paved road turns to gravel in about 2 miles, and swings north. At this writing

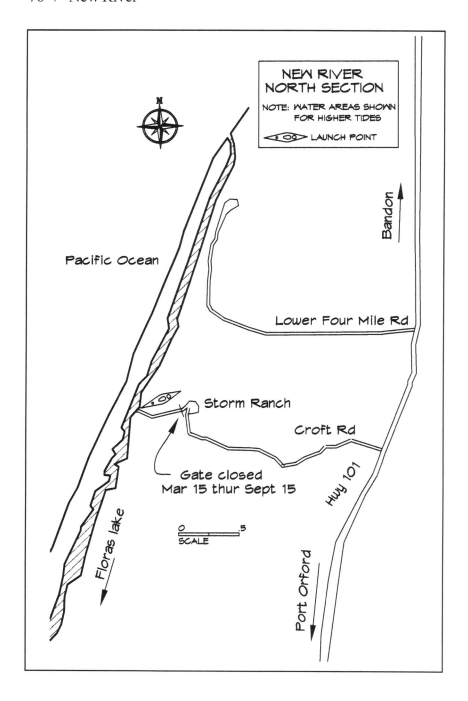

the gravel road ends at a barricade about 1 mile beyond. A sand road continues another 0.5 mile to the edge of New River. This road will eventually be graveled to the edge of New River, providing year-'round access to the north end of the river.

Storm Ranch: From the stoplight in Bandon at US 101 and 11th Ave., go south on US 101 for 8.7 miles. Just beyond milepost 283, turn west on Croft Lake Lane, and follow it 1.6 miles. Take the right fork, following the sign to BLM New River Storm Ranch Area of Critical Environmental Concern. Continue to the Storm Ranch interpretive site. The road beyond Storm Ranch is closed from approximately March 15 to September 15 to protect the threatened western snowy plover's nesting areas. *If the road is closed*: you can park here and portage your vessel the remaining 1 mile to the edge of New River. *If the road is open:* Continue past Storm Ranch and follow the road west, and at a "T" intersection in about 0.4 mile, turn north and follow the road to the parking area at New River. Launch from the river's edge.

Floras Lake: From the stoplight in Bandon at 11th Ave. and US 101, go south on US 101 15 miles to the community of Langlois. Continue south through Langlois and in 0.5 mile turn west on Floras Loop Rd., following signs to Floras Lake and Boice-Cope Park. Continue west, then south, for 1 mile, then turn west on Floras Lake Rd., still following signs to Boice-Cope Park. Continue about 1.6 miles to the park, situated beside Floras Lake. Launch from the public boat ramp or from the point south of the boat ramp. There's a day-use fee.

Facilities/Etc: Restrooms and picnic tables are planned for Four Mile Rd. County Park. Storm Ranch has restrooms, picnic tables at the interpretive center as well as at the river's edge put-in area. Floras Lake has restrooms, picnic tables, campground, bed and breakfast, windsurfing and windsurfing board rentals.

Launch sites: See directions above.

Length: 9 miles (9.85 miles in winter) one way. Floras Lake to Storm Ranch — 6.7 miles. Storm Ranch to Four Mile — 2.2 miles.

Time: 6+ hours

Precautions: Strong north winds must be considered, especially once you get close to the coastline at Floras Creek. Current will also be a factor depending upon the time of year. To avoid these winds, start early and watch for weather patterns. In winter and early spring, when and where the river enters the Pacific Ocean, watch for strong current. It would be wise to exit your boat a bit before the mouth and walk out to it. Paddling may also be difficult as the river will be quite shallow in areas. When the river is connected to the ocean, there will be strong tidal influences. These combined with heavy outflow of water and strong winds from the south may result in some challenging situations!

Discussion: New River is an unusual north-south flowing river created about 100 years ago when a storm carved a new northbound channel for the usually docile Floras Creek. A local rancher supposedly took a look and exclaimed, "It's a new river!" The river is also fed by an outflow of Floras Lake, so you can actually start your tour at the lake, and follow the river 9 or 10 miles north, depending on the time of year and the river's water level. In summer, the river at its northern end narrows and narrows and finally just sort of fizzles out into a flat expanse of beach.. Winter and early spring bring heavy rainfall, along with high surf and tides, and under these conditions New River pushes north another approximately 0.85 mile and carves an outlet to the ocean. That vast expanse of beach becomes a floodplain during high tide.

Such conditions also result in breaches of the dunes in other places along New River, especially near Floras Creek.

The level of the river is seasonally dependent. Best paddling is during sping and early summer months.

From a Floras Lake starting point, the channel is narrow (about 20 feet wide), with the west side sheltered by beachgrass-covered sand dunes. To the east are pasturelands.

At 0.9 mile from Floras Lake is the Floras Creek convergence with New River. The channel becomes much wider, and depending on river levels, there's much more current. Also depending on river levels, you can paddle up Floras Creek for a considerable distance, but again, plan on strong current.

At this point, the river turns west for about 0.4 mile, and nears the Pacific Ocean and sandy beaches. The river becomes quite exposed to north winds at this point. Here also is where the ocean often breaches the sand dunes during stormy winter weather.

Continue to paddle north for about 0.5 mile (distance from beginning = 1.8 miles) where the river narrows again and is separated from the ocean by low dunes, which offer some protection from the wind.

Strong north winds build up waves, some of which will break in the middle of the river. You'll find paddling easier if you stick to the west bank, close to the reeds and grass.

As noted earlier, you can continue for 9 miles to the summertime terminus of New River, or approximately 9.85 miles to its wintertime seaward confluence, or turn around whenever you wish. Paddling back can offer some fun surfing the wind-formed waves. You can also stop and explore the beach to the west, considered one of the most remote in Oregon.

If you want to paddle the entire length of the river to the mouth, consider a shuttle, leaving a vehicle at either the Storm Ranch or Four Mile Rd. site.

Floras Lake

Location: 3 miles southwest of Langlois.

Directions: From US 101 in Langlois, continue south on US 101 about 0.5 mile and turn west on Floras Loop Rd., following signs to Boice-Cope Park. Continue west, then south, for 1 mile, then turn west on Floras Lake Rd., still following signs to Boice-Cope Park.

An early-autumn view looking south from the north end of New River near the Four Mile Road access point. The river ends near here in summer and fall, but in winter continues north 0.85 mile.

Continue about 1.6 miles to the park, situated beside Floras Lake.

Facilities/Etc: Restrooms, picnic tables, campground, pay showers, bed and breakfast, windsurfing rentals. Day use fee for parking in lot next to the lake or in the campground.

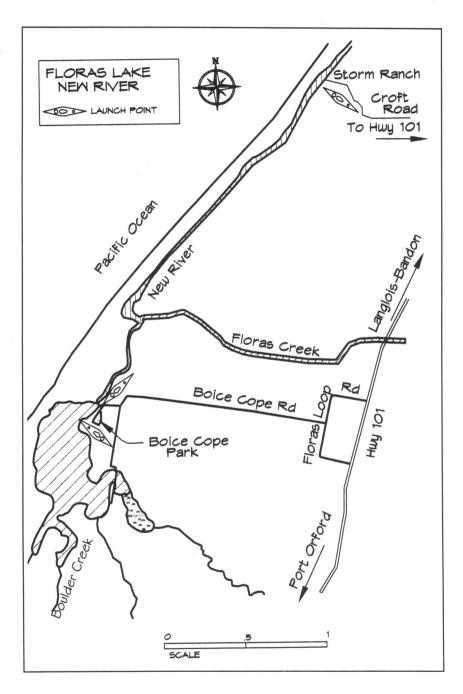

Launch Site: Boat ramp or point of land south of boat ramp.

Length: 4.2 miles (5.2 miles)

Time: 2 hours

Precautions: The north wind can be intense here in summer, so much so that it's become a premier windsurfing destination. Watch for old pilings in places where the sand portion meets the tree line.

Discussion: Floras Lake lies very near the ocean and is a delightful place to paddle. In fact, severe storms have at times breached the berm which separates the ocean from the lake. It is primarily a sand bottom. Paddle across the lake to the ocean side and follow the shoreline around the lake. It has several arms and the shoreline has a great deal of variation. River otters can be often be found near the south end. Depending on the lake level, you can paddle into some wetlands, which are filled with birds. If you paddle early in the morning, you should be able to avoid typical afternoon winds.

Incidentally, the lake is quite shallow in places, especially late in the summer. If you want to practice rolls and rescues, do so near the windsurfing rental, for safety's sake.

John Topits Park/Empire Lakes

Location: In Coos Bay's Empire District, approximately 5 miles from downtown Coos Bay and North Bend.

Directions: From downtown Coos Bay at Anderson St. (Coos Bay Boardwalk), follow US 101 north 1.7 miles and turn west on Newmark Ave. Follow it 1.8 miles and turn north on Hull St., following a sign to John Topits Park/Middle Lake.

Three blocks beyond on Newmark Ave. is Ackerman St., which leads to John Topits Park/Lower Lake.

Facilities/Etc: Lower Lake has restrooms and children's play area.

Facilities/Etc: Lower Lake has restrooms and children's play area.

Launch Site: Boat ramps or sandy beaches.

Length: 3 miles (combined perimeters)

Time: 2 hours

Precautions: Lots of trees, stumps and limbs in the water

Discussion: Lazy paddle in a very picturesque, sheltered area. Birdlife abounds. Good place to practice kayak Eskimo rolls and safety techniques but be aware of water quality. Lower Lake has a bridge you can paddle under into a small arm. Upper/Middle Lake borders Southwestern Oregon Community College. There's an extensive trail system around the lakes.

A canoe awaits further adventure on Empire Lakes.

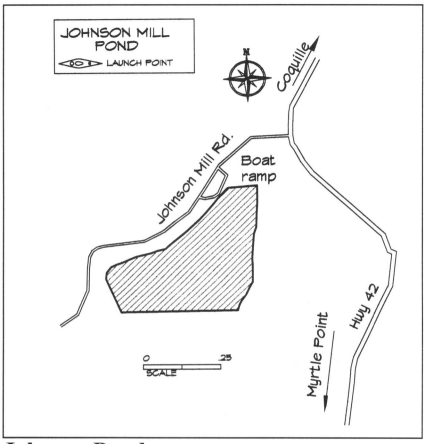

Johnson Pond

Location: 3 miles east of Coquille.

Directions: From Coquille, continue south on Highway 42 2.7 miles and turn right on Johnson Mill Rd.. Follow gravel road to pond.

Facilities/Etc: Restrooms, picnic tables, fishing dock.

Launch Site: Fishing dock.

White-barked alders lean to form a frame for Johnson Pond.

Length: Approximate perimeter is 1.6 miles.

Time: 1 hour.

Precautions: Watch for many old pilings.

Discussion: This is a former storage pond of logs, now used strictly for recreation and wildlife habitat. Birdlife abounds, and there's good fishing from the dock or a canoe.

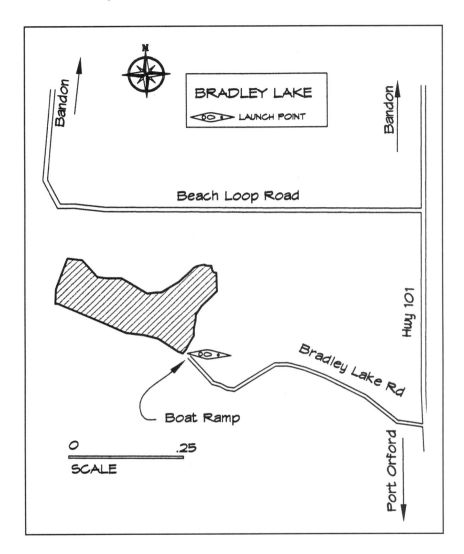

Bradley Lake

Location: 4 miles south of Bandon.

Directions: From the stoplight in Bandon at US 101
and 11th Ave., go south on US 101 3.5 miles and turn west on

Bradley Lake Rd., following is 0.6 mile to boat ramp.

Launch Site: Boat ramp.

Length: 1 mile

Time: 30+ minutes

Precautions: Watch for overhanging limbs and floating debris.

Discussion: Small lake with wetlands. Much of the shoreline is private property. There are some sand dunes at the west end of the lake but are signed as being private property.

Garrison Lake

Location: Port Orford

Directions: From Port Orford, go north on US 101 to 12th St. and turn west, following sign to the public boat ramp. There's an alternate launch site on a road passing by the north end of the lake.

Alternate launch site: From Port Orford, go north on US 101 2 miles and turn west on Paradise Point Rd. Near the end of the road, take a left to an old gravel ramp.

Facilities/Etc: Restrooms, picnic tables at state boat ramp.

Launch Site: See directions above.

Length: 3.8 miles (4.4 miles)

Time: 2+ hours

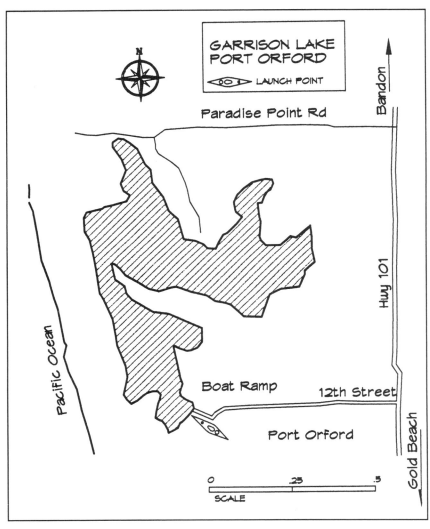

Precautions: The City of Port Orford takes its water from the lake and their intake pipe and pump extends out into the lake at one point. Some old tree limbs and stumps may be a hazard depending upon lake depth. During good weather, wake from recreation boats may be a problem.

Discussion: Fairly shallow lake separated from the ocean by a sand spit. Paddle counter-clockwise and you'll pass custom homes and several inlets to explore. The multitude of birdlife includes egrets and herons. The lake's western shore or "ocean side" has many places to pull up on the sand and explore the beach. The water is very clear and the bottom can be seen in most places.

Powers Pond

Location: Powers County Park, approximately 20 miles southwest of Myrtle Point.

Directions: From Highway 42 in Myrtle Point, continue east about 3 miles and take the turnoff to Powers. Continue about 18 miles to Powers County Park, on the west end of town.

Facilities/Etc: Restrooms, picnic area, children's play area, campground.

Launch site: Boat ramp or grassy embankment.

Length: 1 mile.

Time: 1 hour.

Precautions: Watch for anglers.

Discussion: Another one-time log storage pond, this 40-acre lake offers easy paddling. Lake is stocked with trout and open for fishing year-'round.

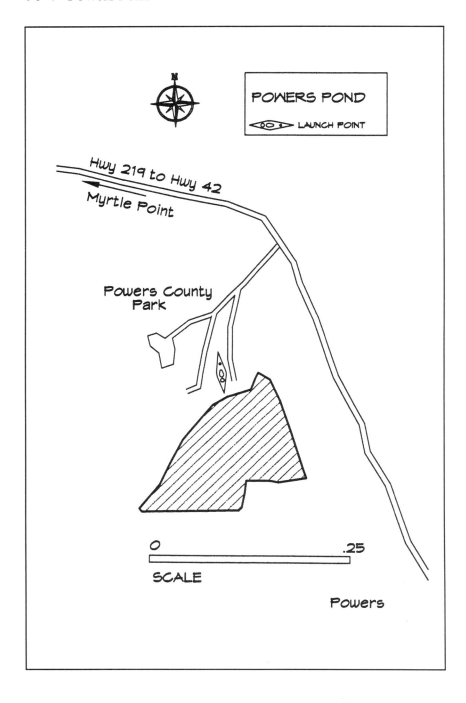

Ben Irving Reservoir

Location: Near Tenmile, approximately 10 miles west of Winston.

Directions: Just west of Tenmile along Highway 42, turn left on Benedict Rd. near milepost 64, following the sign to Ben Irving Reservoir. (Eastbound travelers on Highway 42 can turn on Ireland Rd. near milepost 62, and follow signs to the reservoir.)

Facilities/Etc: Restrooms, picnic tables.

Launch Site: Boat ramp or sandy areas.

Length: 3.8+ miles

Time: 2 hours

Precautions: Some stumps and limbs in the water. Paddling to the left of the boat ramp will lead into an area of high-speed boats.

Discussion: I've included this paddle because if you're driving to or from the Coos Bay Area on Highway 42, it's a really nice place to take a "paddle break." From the boat ramp and docks, the left end of the lake is used primarily by power boaters. The right end of the lake has restrictions on it. 0.3 mile from the ramp, a 5 mile-per- hour restriction begins. At 0.8 mile from the ramp, a no-motor restriction begins and continues to the end of the lake. This is the best section to paddle. You could add another 3 miles to the tour by paddling the left section. Do so early in the morning or during the week in summertime. Little boat traffic will be found in the winter and early spring.

The lake is narrow in parts and many signs warn of stumps. Near the right end of the lake, you'll find a freshwater wetland area with many birds and waterfowl.

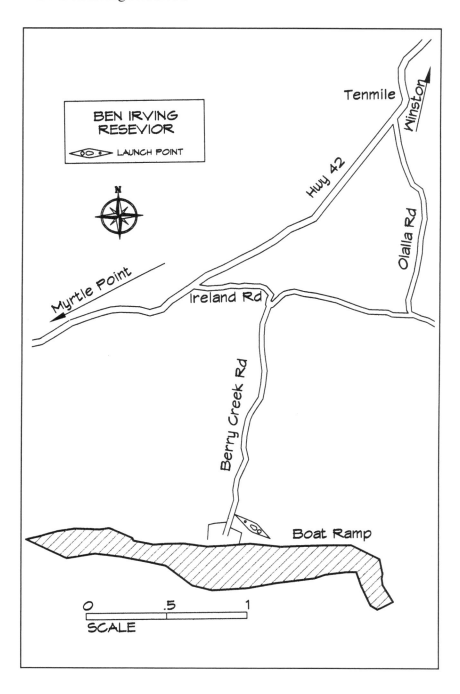

GLOBAL POSITIONING SYSTEM COORDINATES

For the techno people, here are the GPS coordinates for the various launches.

Ben Irving Reservoir
43.02.936
123.34.025

North Bend Boat Ramp
43.24.466
124.13.257

North Spit Launch Point
43.26.252
124.14.184

Rocky Point
43.09.791
124.21.706

Shinglehouse Slough
43.19.529
124.12.384

Bandon
43.07.208
124.24.721

Bullards Beach State Park Boat Ramp
43.08.851
124.24.066

Davis Slough
43.17.304
124.13.675

Empire Boat Ramp
43.23.542
124.16.794

Charleston/Charleston Shipyard (TV Beach)
43.20.178
124.15.121

Coquille Sturdivant Park
42.24.885
124.16.804

Eastside Boat Ramp
43.21.813
124.12.352

Greenacres Boat Ramp
43.15.365
124.12.852

Garrison Lake
43.34.390
124.10.250

Floras Lake
42.54.072
124.30.126

Eel Lake
43.36.243
124 .10.577

North Spit Boat Ramp
43.24.891
124.16.767

Storm Ranch
42.59.810
124.27.423

Summer/Fall end New Rive
43.01.496
124.26.858

Saunders Lake
43.31.825
124.13.007

HELPFUL PHONE NUMBERS

US Coast Guard, Charleston (non emergency) (541) 888-3266
Marine weather: (541) 888-3102   Aviation weather: (541) 756-0135
South Slough National Estuarine Research Reserve (541) 888-5558
Bay Area Chamber of Commerce, Coos Bay (541) 269-0215
Bandon Visitors' Center (541) 347-9616   Port of Bandon (541) 347-3206
Oregon Int'l. Port of Coos Bay, Charleston Marina (541) 888-2548
Adventure Kayak, Bandon (541) 347-3480
Hightide Rental, Charleston (541) 888-3664
Coos County Parks, Coquille (541) 396-3121 ext. 354
Oregon Dunes National Recreation Area, Reedsport (541) 271-3611
Oregon State Parks, Southwestern Division (541) 888-8867

ABOUT THE AUTHOR

Ron Wardman is a longtime resident and paddler in Oregon's Coos Region, recently retired from a 30-year career teaching technical and vocational classes at Myrtle Point High School. He also operates an architectural drafting business.

A native of Colorado, Ron attended the University of North Colorado, and received a master's degree from Western Oregon State College. He accepted a teaching position in Oregon to be near the Pacific Ocean and the many other outdoor opportunities of the region. He continues to pursue lifelong interests in kayaking, windsurfing, boating, sailing, mountain biking,hiking and motorcycling.

He's built a number of sailboats, as well as a redwood-stripped canoe. He's pictured on the cover and in most of the other kayaking photos in the book.

NOTE FROM THE AUTHOR

I would like to give special thanks to my editor and publisher, Tom Baake. I met him at a local trails meeting and mentioned my tour book in progress. He offered to help me complete it. My vision was a rather simple guidebook but he helped me make it a much better and more usable book for paddlers. Ken Cook supplied the base maps of the Coos Region.

I'd also like to thank fellow paddlers Dick Vigue, Reed Lockhart and Pastor Terry Dill ,who joined me on many of these the tours. Also thanks to Ned Reed for information about the Coquille River.

FOR YOUR INFORMATION

Get continuous weather info on VHF radio by tuning to 162.4 mHz

The National Data Buoy Center maintains a weather station at Cape Arago that is connected to the Internet with continuously updated information on weather, wind and other conditions. The URL is:

http://www.ndbc.noaa.gov/station_page.phtml?$station=caro3

NOTE FROM THE PUBLISHER

Your help is very much appreciated! If you have comments or suggestions for future editions, please let us know. If you find any mistakes, we need to hear about those as well.

Updated information about paddling in the Coos Region will be posted on our web site, and you can find information about other books published by Westways Press, including "Out Our Back Door, Driving Tours and Hiking Trails in the Coos Region."

Just go to www.scod.com/guidebooks.

Send comments, suggestions or orders for additional copies to:

Westways Press
440 Third Ct.
Coos Bay, OR 97420
(541) 269-5833
e-mail: tbaake@harborside.com

Find out more about recreational opportunities in the Coos Region by visiting the Internet web site: www.coostrails.com.

ABOUT THE PHOTOS & ARTWORK

Many thanks to Peggy O'Neal/WOW Arts and Exhibits of North Bend and to Deb Matson of Coos Bay for the use of original artwork in this book.

All photos were taken by Tom Baake, and many depict the author paddling in the various locales described. On the cover is a photo looking east from the North Spit launch point, described on page 32. In the background is McCullough Bridge, perhaps the most recognizable landmark of the Coos Bay Area. The frontispiece photo is of Lone Rock, in Haynes Inlet, described on page 42.

Thanks to Frank Babcock for bringing out his handmade cedar canoe for some of the photos.

Thanks to Kate Fieland and to all the other folks who let us use photos of them.

Destination:

Location:

Directions:

Facilities/Etc:

Launch site:

Length:

Time:

Precautions:

Discussion:

Got paddles?